31 DAYS FOR
ADVENT
FOR SMALL GROUP
OR PERSONAL USE

CW00675565

Heralding
the coming **King**

CWR

Anne Calver

Copyright © CWR 2016

Published 2016 by CWR, Waverley Abbey House, Waverley Lane, Farnham, Surrey GU9 8EP, UK.
Registered Charity No. 294387. Registered limited company No. 1990308.

The right of Anne Calver to be identified as the author of this work has been asserted by her in
accordance with the Copyright, Designs and Patents Act 1988, sections 77 and 78.

For a list of National Distributors, visit www.cwr.org.uk/distributors

Unless otherwise indicated, all Scripture references are from the Holy Bible, New International Version®
Anglicised, NIV® Copyright © 1979, 1984, 2011 by Biblica, Inc.® Used by permission. All rights reserved
worldwide.

Every effort has been made to ensure that this book contains the correct permissions and references,
but if anything has been inadvertently overlooked, the Publisher will be pleased to make the
necessary arrangements at the first opportunity. Please contact the Publisher directly.

Concept development, editing, design and production by CWR

Cover image: adobe.com

Printed in the UK by Linney Group.

ISBN: 978-1-78259-521-2

Contents

Introduction

Using the faithful narrative in the Gospels of Matthew and Luke, let's consider the journeys of the central figures at the heart of Advent. Through looking afresh at the lives of key people, such as the magi, shepherds, Mary, Joseph and Herod, we can unpack some of their character and decisions, asking the Lord to apply the godly aspects of each to our personal journey today.

At the heart of it all is a baby – the King of kings, Jesus Christ – and every daily reading will point towards Him. My hope is that you will be able to seek the face of Jesus in a new way.

The first section is entitled 'Prepare the way' and will take a brief look at the Gospel authors Matthew and Luke and how they reveal the truth of God to His people. Zechariah and Elizabeth, the parents of John the Baptist, point and prepare us for the arrival of the Messiah – teaching us to dream bigger dreams, believe for more and expect the unexpected with God.

The second section, 'Drawing near to Jesus', is about encountering and developing a relationship with Him. We will delve into the text surrounding Mary and Joseph to consider how they drew near to God and trusted Him with everything they had. This section will also cover Simeon's prophetic announcements and intimacy with God and ask us what we can implement from their experiences into our own lives.

The third section takes us another step towards Christ, encouraging us to 'Seek Him first' – putting Him above everything else. We will begin with Anna and her personal intimacy with the Lord. Moving on to the magi and the shepherds, we will discover how they were willing to lay down their plans, follow a star and journey for months, all because they knew this King was worth seeking first.

Finally, the fourth section asks the challenging question: 'Who will you live for?' Interestingly we will consider Herod and how his decisions made it clear he was only living for himself. Could we be in danger of doing the same? We end with a clear focus on the One who lies at the heart of it all – Jesus; remembering who He is, what He has done for us and deciding whether we will give everything to live for Him.

My prayer is that you will encounter not just a baby in a manger but a risen Saviour, who can speak and minister to us today as powerfully as He did to those living thousands of years ago. The Advent season is a time to discover more of who Jesus really is, raising our faith and believing that He is at work in us and through us to transform lives, not just in Judea, but wherever we live now. Be blessed!

How to use this book

This guide is designed to be read day by day, alongside the Bible. There are thirty-one days so you may choose to read it in the month of December, over the Christmas period, but it has been left undated so that you can also pick it up at any time. It has also been separated into four different sections to structure your reading and help you to consider your relationship with Jesus and how you can seek Him more.

Each day begins with an opening prayer to focus on the day's topic and to prepare you to meet with the Lord through His Word. This is followed by the appropriate Bible reading and notes to expand on the person mentioned in the passage. Each day also suggests a further reading to ponder, questions to consider and a reflection, to help you apply the study to your own life.

If you are using this book in a small group, it will work well if members have an individual copy to read throughout the week. Then, as you complete each section, you can use the Group Study Notes at the back of the book to discuss and consolidate what you have learnt.

ONE

Prepare the way

Matthew 1:1-25; Luke 1:1-25

DAY 1

Behind the scenes

Opening prayer

Lord, we thank You for the Gospel writers, and the way that they draw us deeper into Your living truth. Please reveal Yourself more to me, as I consider Your Word. Amen.

Bible reading

Matthew 1:1–25

As we begin to walk through the Advent season, and meet the people surrounding Christ in His early moments, we cannot help but consider the writers who bring the story to life. Both Luke and Matthew are deeply concerned to communicate the truth of the events surrounding the birth of Jesus. Although not an eyewitness, Luke has widely researched what has happened and is so familiar with the details that he is able to present a witness that is believed to be very close to what actually came about. Matthew, on the other hand, wants to begin his Gospel by stressing the reality that Jesus was indeed a descendant of King David, answering and fulfilling the prophetic utterances of the Old Testament. By beginning with the genealogy, Matthew wants his Jewish readers to see the history leading up to Jesus and therefore the truth that He is indeed the Messiah. Both our writers are keen to really look at and understand what happened as Jesus entered the world.

So often Christmas passes us by in a manic rush and many of us are relieved when it is over! Perhaps our memories are filled with bin liners of torn wrappings or scraps of turkey that even the dog wasn't able to finish! Maybe we are happy to recall good chats around the fire and journeys to relatives that are, in our normal day-to-day, a rare thing. The interesting thing is that Christmas is still marked as a special time of year; it may have lost a lot of its meaning to most, but it is thankfully still set aside as an annual holiday and we are encouraged to stop before entering a new year.

However, the narrative in Luke and Matthew can feel like a world away from our modern-day 'Christmas experience'. For some of us, the only glimpse of the Messiah is through a carol service, a school nativity, a service or perhaps from carol singers at the shopping centre. I believe that Jesus wants to show us more than that this Advent, and every Christmas. He is wanting to reveal Himself to you in such a way that His life is not restricted to a moment, but rather is dug up, fully considered and able to transform our lives.

Instead of just stopping when the holidays come, can you carve out a time to pause each day in order to put Christ at the very centre of the Christmas craziness? Allow Him to change your perspective, to touch and change your life afresh, so that as you pass the stressed out consumers you can show them another way. Remember the King is coming. Are we ready for Him?

Ponder
Romans 12:1–2

Questions to consider
- Are you ready and willing to go deeper with Christ?
- Maybe it is time to ask the Lord Jesus to minister to you in a new way this Advent?

Reflect
Offer yourself afresh to the Lord, considering the verse, 'Be still, and know that I am God' (Psa. 46:10).

DAY 2

A right spirit

Opening prayer

Lord, as I consider Zechariah's 'right spirit', please speak to me about my life and give me the strength to live the way that You are calling me to. Amen.

Bible reading

Luke 1:5–23

We read that the priest Zechariah and his wife Elizabeth were both 'righteous in the sight of God, observing all the Lord's commands and decrees blamelessly' (Luke 1:6). What an amazing sentence to read about someone! Imagine if someone said that you were a 'righteous and blameless' person, and not just in their eyes, but in the eyes of God.

The Lord must have been so thrilled with the way that Zechariah and Elizabeth dedicated their lives to His service. With Zechariah we see someone who would have longed to give his wife a child, a guy who was getting on in years and had not received everything he wanted in life and yet lived righteously. Zechariah was a righteous man – He was right with the Lord. We don't read that he moaned or turned his back on the King, rather He continued in this faithful observance of all His commandments. He was blameless.

This man entered the Temple with a pure heart and was ready to meet with God; little did he realise what awaited him! He was the first to be told that the plan for the coming King was in motion. I wonder how much Zechariah's faithfulness led him to his encounter with the angel.

It is interesting to consider why Luke emphasises the godliness of Zechariah and Elizabeth. When you think of someone who is blameless, you think of a person who never does anything wrong, an individual who honours God in thought, word and deed. The Lord sees this couple and their spotless lives and chooses them.

The truth is that we will never be blameless, otherwise Jesus would not have needed to die; however, He does long that we will become more like Him. He does not choose us because we abide by the law and do good because we have to; He appoints us because we love Him and seek to live lives that honour Him.

During a time of prayer at church recently, I had a deep sense in my spirit that the Lord was smiling on this part of His body. Then, following the warm smile, the word 'faithfulness' sprung into my mind. Under my breath I said, 'Lord, have we been faithful to you?' And I felt Him say 'Yes, and your faithfulness is going to lead to great fruitfulness'. A couple of weeks later another word came to the Church pastor from a leader who said, 'Get ready for the harvest to come in'. His word backed up the sense that I had experienced and it was so exciting!

Yes, the Lord is gracious to us sinners, but I also believe that He looks at the heart and He longs for children of faithfulness, like Zechariah – those who remain committed, whatever the cost, and no matter what we have to give up.

Ponder
Titus 2:11–12; 1 Peter 1:6–7

Questions to consider
- Are you being faithful to the Lord?
- Would He describe your walk with Him as blameless?
- Is there anything that He is asking you to change?

Reflect
Surrender everything to Jesus, asking Him to help you to live a life that looks like His.

A moment of doubt

Opening prayer

Lord Jesus, thank You that when You make promises to Your children they always come to pass – even if they happen in a way that I do not expect. Help me to trust You with my whole life. Amen.

Bible reading

Luke 1:18–20

Thank goodness that, even in his righteousness, Zechariah was not perfect! Even this godly, right-spirited man had moments of doubt. The angel came to him with the news that Elizabeth would bear a child but Zechariah responded with; 'How can I be sure of this?' (v18). You can't really blame him for being puzzled, both he and his wife were far from being sprightly, young things, they were in fact 'well on in years' (v18), and yet the angel told him that they would have a child! We cannot help but hear echoes of Moses' questioning when he met God at the burning bush. The Lord told him to ask Pharoah to let His people go, and Moses was terrified. He responded with, but 'what if they do not believe me or listen to me and say, "The LORD did not appear to you"?' (Exod. 4:1). Even being visited by an angel of the Lord or hearing His voice in a burning bush is not quite enough! Both men are filled with questions of doubt, and this is not unusual in Scripture.

As you read the narrative, part of you thinks, 'But look, Zechariah, you are witnessing the glory of the Lord, how on earth can you still be doubting?!' But then we quickly remember that these guys were people, just like you and me. They were human and even in the face of encounter, their earthly minds still influenced their thinking.

It reminds me of a friend of mine who says that whenever she is just about to get up and preach about the goodness of God and declare the truth of who He is, a little thought pops into her mind, 'But what if all this is not true?'. It is like a snag of the enemy, a last ditch attempt to stop her from speaking the truth of the Word to mankind. And yet she still gets up and declares the truth of the gospel of Christ. Interestingly, she then clearly witnesses the Lord move in power. Encounter does not mean that we never doubt.

Zechariah, like Moses, and like you and me, struggled and found himself questioning – what about this, that and the other? We all have questions and uncertainty, but what will we do with these doubts? Zechariah chose to believe what the angel was saying to him and everything that was declared over his life came to pass, as it did for Elizabeth, Joseph, Mary and Moses. God is faithful, we just have to trust Him. He may ask us to do something that seems as crazy as having a baby in the late years of life, but if it is Him saying it, He will bring it about.

Ponder
Proverbs 3:5–6

Questions to consider
- Can you trust God?
- Zechariah asked, 'How can I be sure of this?' Are you also looking for a sign so that you can be certain about which way to walk or what decision to make?
- What do you believe God says in response?

Reflect
Read the words from Psalm 86:5–13, proclaiming and trusting in His love.

DAY 4

A sense of fear

Opening prayer

Prince of Peace, please help me to overcome my fear. I do not want it to limit who I am and what You want to do in and through my life. Please make me willing to be faithful to You. Amen.

Bible reading

Luke 1:11–13

I remember chatting with a guy who was hungry for the presence of the Lord. He was always going forwards for prayer, He would wait patiently in prayer times to see what Jesus was saying to him. He spent hours in his Bible, asking the Lord to speak to him through Scripture and was passionate about ministry in the power of the Holy Spirit. There came a point where the Holy Spirit was drawing him into deeper intimacy with Jesus and so every time he was being prayed for, he could feel the front of his feet lifting off the floor and he knew that if he was willing, that he could simply fall flat on his back. But something stopped him. Every time. He felt afraid. There was a fear of a loss of control, a fear of hurting himself and more than that, a fear of what the Lord would require of him if he was slain in the Spirit. He loved the Lord with all of his heart but the presence of the King to this extent was too much for him. He resisted falling but remains a faithful servant of Jesus.

When we read this part of Zechariah's story, I find echoes of a similar spirit. A faithful, righteous man, obeying the Lord in everything and seeking His face in the temple; however, when the presence of God comes in power, Zechariah is startled and gripped with fear. Suddenly there was a loss of control and order to his ritual life and he is led down a path of vulnerability that was to prove life changing.

The reality is that Zechariah had absolutely nothing to be afraid of and the angel is clear about that. In fact, the angel is there to tell him that his prayers and longings have been answered. This is such a good reminder that when we are pressing the Lord for something, we may have to face and overcome our fear to receive what we long for. The truth of the matter is that fear will keep us stuck where we are. The Lord will not force us, He works with us where we are, but He longs to show us more than what we see.

In that old childhood game where you fall backwards and someone catches you, there is very little fear. However, I wonder how many of us would be willing to fall back and trust someone to catch us now we have grown up? It is a bit like Peter walking on water. He steps out of what is comfortable and becomes afraid, but then he fixes his eyes on Jesus and is saved (Matt. 14:22–33). Let's not let fear cripple us as we push into all that the Lord has in store for our lives.

Ponder
Matthew 14:22–33

Questions to consider
• What are you afraid of?
• Do you fear God?
• Did Zechariah need to be afraid?
• Is it time to overcome your fear and go out into deeper water?

Reflect
Read Psalm 96 aloud, with particular emphasis on verses 4–6.

DAY 5

Nothing is impossible

Opening prayer

Heavenly Father, thank You for showing us that nothing is impossible with You. Even if we have given up hope, You can do miraculous things. Please help us to turn our longings into prayers. Amen.

Bible reading

Luke 1:5–25,37

The angel declared that Elizabeth would have a baby, and she subsequently defied her old age by falling pregnant and giving birth to a son, John the Baptist. She must have been absolutely amazed as she watched her mute husband, her belly swelling and people around her questioning what had happened. She had been an older lady, with a longing in her heart (which she had probably given up believing would ever happen) and then all of a sudden, the great and awesome Lord most High gave her the one thing that she believed was impossible to have, a baby. And this was not just any baby; this child would prepare the way for the Lord Jesus.

Quite often when we want something we will share our desire with other people. We may pray about our longing with close friends or family. We sometimes do things to try and get what we want – such as changing where we live, going on dating websites, trying IVF or moving jobs. Then after a while, when things don't seem to really change, we go quiet about the thing that we long for. Maybe we even stop praying about it, because it becomes too painful to even utter. Those around us know what we long for, but they stop talking to us about it because they know it hurts. In extreme circumstances, perhaps we even start to feel like the one that they talk about to one another.

When we consider Elizabeth, we see someone who knew what it was like to long for something. She had no doubt spent hours in prayer alone and with her family and friends. She, like some of us, will have got to an age where people just stopped talking to her about children because it was 'never going to be'. I wonder how uncomfortable she felt around her peers who had raised families and how she handled the pain of not having the child she longed for.

And then, out of nowhere, something changed! All human understanding suggested that this baby would never *ever* be a reality for Zechariah and Elizabeth, but God's reply was: *'Nothing is impossible with me!'* When Jesus goes to the tomb to raise Lazarus from the dead, He says, 'Our friend Lazarus has fallen asleep; but I am going there to wake him up' (John 11:11). God's view of a situation is entirely different to ours! Jesus is effectively saying, 'This is no big deal, I will just go and wake him'.

That person you are praying for; that situation that you believe will never change; that longing in your heart that will not go away – do not give up. Our ways are not God's ways and what He does will be different to what we planned, but do not lose hope in Christ. Keep praying and seeking His face as Elizabeth did. He is with you.

Ponder
Romans 8:22–27

Questions to consider
- Are you living with longing?
- Are you able to pray about what you long for?
- Can you ask the Lord to renew your hope in Him?

Reflect
Meditate on 2 Timothy 2:1,11–12.

DAY 6

God is faithful

Opening prayer

Lord Jesus, thank You for being faithful to me in so many ways. Please open my eyes to give thanks and remember all that You have done and are doing for me. Amen.

Bible reading

Luke 1:25,57–58

Regarding her pregnancy, Elizabeth exclaimed, 'In these days he has shown his favour and taken away my disgrace among the people'. Note Elizabeth's words, 'In these days' (v25) – not before, not after, but at just the appointed time, God showed His favour and she had a baby boy. Elizabeth could have fallen pregnant at another time in a different way, she could have remained childless for the rest of her life; the Lord still loved her no matter what. However, there was a bigger picture at work, a story of salvation, a preparing of the way of the Lord, which was being worked out according to the Lord's plan, not a human agenda. Yes, this child brought Elizabeth, her family, her friends and neighbours great joy because the Lord had shown His mercy, but there wassomething else happening here. This child was not just a blessing to Zechariah and Elizabeth but a blessing for the whole world.

God's timing is so interesting and so different to ours. This couple could not see and understand why they were having a baby 'in these days' because they only saw a tiny picture compared to what the Lord could see. Think about Lazarus when he was sick, and his sisters, Martha and Mary, begging Jesus to come and heal him, what did Jesus do? Interestingly, He stayed where He was for two days (John 11:6). By the time that Jesus reached the weeping sisters, His friend and their brother had been dead in the tomb for four days. In the eyes and understanding of these precious ladies, they must have been furious with Jesus (John 11:21) and Jesus too was very sad (John 11:33,35,38). However, the Father's timing and perspective is different to theirs and at that moment, 'in this day', Jesus publically raised Lazarus from the dead (subsequently signing His own death warrant, because only God can give and take away life). In doing this He showed those witnessing the event that He truly was, and is, the Son of the Most High God.

There is always a bigger picture at work than what we see. God saved Lazarus not just for his sisters, but as a signal to the rest of the world. God gave Elizabeth a baby not just to give her the joy of motherhood, but to prepare the way for the true King of the Jews. Often God honours His people in a time and in a way that we cannot predict. God is faithful to His children and He will never leave us or forsake us. Even in the waiting, He feels our pain and sees us where we are. He loves us.

Ponder
John 11:1–44

Questions to consider
- Have you considered the bigger picture of your circumstances?
- Why not ask the Lord to begin to show you more of what He is unveiling?
- What has Jesus saved you from?

Reflect
Read Ecclesiastes 3:1–8,11, asking God to help you to accept His perfect timing.

DAY 7

Give glory to God

Opening prayer

Holy One, please help me to remember what You have done for me. I desire to be someone who doesn't just ask, but also gives thanks and praise to You each day. Thank You for saving me, Jesus. Amen.

Bible reading

Luke 1:25,45

I wonder what percentage of the population pray for things during their life time? It seems that many people pray when they are seriously ill, or know someone who is poorly. Other people pray for houses and jobs, some ask God for children and many of these people might not call themselves followers of Christ. There are also many Christians who pray for all of the above but also add prayers for other people to meet Jesus and for the Lord to move in many more circumstances. Some of us might even confess to asking God for car parking spaces, especially when we are in a hurry!

The challenge we have is that we are often happy to ask God for what we want but sadly may not be as quick to thank God when He answers and provides for us. Even more than that, how many of us are not only personally and privately grateful for what the Lord has given, but are willing to publicly praise and thank God for all that He has done?

I remember knowing that the Lord was challenging me on this very subject. My husband and I went through an incredibly tough journey in having children and I knew, after giving birth to a son at 31 weeks, that I had to find a way to give glory to God! Due to antibodies, our son had gone through nine blood transfusions in the womb from 17 weeks onwards. The risk each time was brain damage or heart attack and for a foetus that small, it was terrifying. We clung to the Lord and felt Him say that the baby was called Daniel because He was protecting him from the mouths of the lions. The joy that we experienced when he was declared fit and well was the most incredible feeling that we have been privileged to feel. When Daniel was one year old we had a party and a service of thanksgiving for him. We invited the man who had safely performed the transfusions in utero and delivered our son. Surrounded by close family and friends we publicly gave glory to God for the gift of Daniel and how He had led us through this incredibly difficult time in our lives.

Elizabeth too gave glory to God! She did not ignore what had happened or suggest that she was just 'lucky'; instead she declares 'The Lord has done this' (v25). We all have a choice to declare God's glory – His favour, His goodness and His provision. We can argue it away, we can pretend it is no big deal, or we can attribute it to Him, privately and publicly. There is great power in witnessing to what He has done for us.

Ponder
Daniel 6:21–28

Questions to consider
- When you ask the Lord to do something, are you quick to thank Him afterwards?
- Have you ever publicly recognised the way God has answered your prayers?
- What difference does it make to your faith?

Reflect
Read these verses and give thanks to God for all He has done:
Psalm 148:2–3; 150:1–3; 109:30.

TWO

Draw near to Jesus

Luke 1:26-38; 2:25-35; Matthew 1:18-25

DAY 8

Put Jesus first

Opening prayer

Lord, thank You for Mary and the way that she was willing to say yes to You, despite the cost. Please help me to focus on You above all else, and say yes to You. Amen.

Bible reading

Luke 1:26–38

Mary, the mother of Jesus, is truly remarkable. She is visited by an angel who tells her that the power from the Most High will overshadow her and that she will give birth to the son of God! Yes, she questions and she is afraid like Zechariah, but after hearing all that the angel has to say, Mary's response is mind-blowing: 'I am the Lord's servant ... may your word to me be fulfilled' (Luke 1:38).

You may ask why this is such an incredible line of scripture. The reasons are extensive, but, in particular, this response from the mother of Christ shows us how much godliness and obedience there was in her character. Mary is prepared to put all her doubts, fears, expectations and plans aside, and to say 'yes' to God. She knew that the pregnancy would bring her disgrace; she knew Joseph would not believe her and would think that she had been with another man. She also knew that this might mean that she would remain unmarried and cast out of society. Could it get much worse than that for a woman in those days? A single, disgraced, isolated, rejected young woman with a story that surely no one in their right mind was going to believe! And yet this teenage girl was prepared to put God's plans ahead of her own – she put God first.

When we read about the prophet Isaiah and his utterances regarding the arrival of the Messiah, we discover a man who was a bit like Mary. He encounters the Lord in a powerful way and, before he is commissioned, turns to the Lord and says, 'Here am I. Send me!' (Isa. 6:8). Isaiah is open and willing to put his life into God's hands and to put His will above his own. Both Isaiah and Mary show us a deep dependency and trust in the Lord. They know that God's way is the best way to live and their obedience reveals hearts that are totally submitted to Him.

Both Mary and Isaiah had no idea what their 'yes' to God would lead to, but they still said it and lived it out. I wonder whether we are prepared to say 'yes' to God's will for us and to put His agenda first in everything that we do. Perhaps we struggle to trust that if we truly submit to Christ, He will really have a better plan for our lives than we do. It is a simple thing to say, 'Yes, Lord, I put you first' but another thing altogether to live like that. We need the power of God to equip us and you can guarantee that He will give us all the strength necessary for the task at hand.

Ponder
Matthew 6:33

Questions to consider
- What comes first in your life?
- Could you have said 'yes' to God like Mary did?
- Is God challenging you to change your order of priorities?
  If so, how?

Reflect
Turn Matthew 6:33 into a personal prayer to Jesus: 'Help us to seek Your kingdom and Your righteousness first, and trust that everything else will be added to us. Amen.'

DAY 9

Don't limit yourself

Opening prayer

Oh Lord, thank You for making me unique. Thank You that I am special to You. Help me to understand more of Your love for me and not limit myself. Amen.

Bible reading

Luke 1:28,30

I grew up subconsciously believing that men were in charge of the family and that it was the father figure who made all the final big decisions – especially if they were financially driven! When I think about it now, I realise that my mum actually ran the home and made most of the decisions, but there was this underlying understanding that my dad was where the buck stopped. It was the same at my church; I believed in men in leadership and in women having roles that supported them and helped them to do the best job they could do. So when I got married, I carried this belief with me – God had given me my husband Gavin and I needed to support, release, sacrifice and complement him; enabling him to be the best he could be in leadership. Being a wife and a mother was my role.

Now please don't misunderstand me – I still passionately believe in enabling and supporting my husband; I was raised in an incredible home and I respect those with a different understanding. However, in my journey I recognise now that I had limited myself. Without realising it, I had decided my role and limited what God might want to say and do with me. I had definitely thought much less of myself than Jesus wanted me to!

When the angel of the Lord says to Mary, 'Greetings, you who are highly favoured!' (v28) and 'you have found favour with God' (v30), you can hear Him saying; 'You may think you are nothing and no one, but I see you, and my plan for you is a million times more amazing than you have imagined'. The Lord's love for His children liberates them from their human understanding, opens their eyes to possibility and takes them to places they never imagined.

When the Lord spoke Acts 2:18 over me: 'Even on my servants, both men and women, I will pour out my Spirit in those days, and they will prophesy', I had an intense experience of the power of God. I knew God was saying, 'This is not just about Gavin, but you too, Anne. Don't limit me and my power through you'. Soon after I felt led to explore ordination.

Mary suddenly has a deep understanding of the Lord's love for her, which causes her to glorify God in song: Luke 1:46–56. She has a sudden deep awareness of God and His plans for the world and His heart for the poor. After her encounter with the angel, Mary's perspective on life shifts significantly.

I truly believe that the Lord longs to liberate us – breaking through the limits we cover ourselves with – and leading us into a life with Him that we never dreamt or imagined was possible.

Ponder
Acts 2:14–18

Questions to consider
- In what ways do you limit yourself?
- Why do you do this?
- What lies are you believing?
- Why not ask the Spirit of the living God to fall afresh on you today, revealing His truth?

Reflect
Consider the words in Psalm 139:13–18 and let them soak into your soul.

DAY 10

Let the Spirit come

Opening prayer

Lord, thank You that You didn't leave us alone, but that You sent Your Spirit to us. Please help us to know His transforming power at work in our lives each day. Amen.

Bible reading

Luke 1:35

Imagine the Lord telling you, 'The Holy Spirit will come upon you and the power of the Most High will overshadow you' (Luke 1:35) – how would that make you feel? Perhaps you agree that there is something exciting and yet scary about it. Often there is a sense of fear in relation to the unknown. We don't actually know how scared Mary felt when she conceived the Son of God, or exactly how it happened. All the angel tells us is that the Spirit would come to her and then she would fall pregnant, but Scripture does not narrate the power of the Most High overshadowing her, so even now what exactly happened is still unknown.

We can have all kinds of reactions to the Holy Spirit – some of us are open and desperate to experience more of God, others may be sceptical and careful. Some promote the Father and the Son but struggle with the third part of the Trinity. There are some groups and individuals that struggle to let go of control and are afraid of the power of the Holy Spirit. Whoever you are and however you may feel about the Holy Spirit, the angel's message is clear: for the Son of God to come into the world, the Spirit is necessary to bring it about.

God encounters His children, shares His heart and plans for them and equips and anoints them by the power of the Holy Spirit, in order to accomplish His purposes in and through their lives. The Holy Spirit is given to help us in our weakness, not to scare us. He is there to reveal truth to us, so that we don't walk around clouded by lies. The Spirit gives us boldness and courage to speak up and act for the sake of the kingdom, rather than remain confined and limited. Nothing the Spirit does is meant to terrify us but rather enlighten, guide and strengthen us at every turn.

I remember my dad telling me a story of a conversation he had once with someone who used to practise witchcraft. He was working in the bar of the hotel that he ran at the time when this person began chatting very openly with him. During the course of conversation, after realising that my dad was a Christian, she commented; 'you Christians don't realise the power that you have'. She told my dad that she used to walk past Christians and know that they were followers of Jesus because they would 'glow'. She knew that the power they had was greater than the power of darkness and wondered why they didn't use and share it more.

When Jesus ascended into heaven, He promised to send the Holy Spirit and when the Spirit came, the disciples' lives were transformed upside down and back to front. Remember, this power is available to all of us.

Ponder
1 Thessalonians 1:4–5; Luke 11:13; John 14:25–27; Galatians 5:18

Questions to consider
- What is your reaction to the Holy Spirit?
- Do you feel open to let the Holy Spirit guide you through life?
- Why not ask the Spirit to empower you with what you need for the tasks that lie ahead today?

Reflect
Read Psalm 104 aloud, with particular emphasis on verses 27–30.

DAY 11

Doing the right thing

Opening prayer

Heavenly Father, thank You for the example of the saints who were willing to do what was right, even when it was deeply costly to them and their loved ones. Please help us to do what is right and to be open to change in the right direction. Amen.

Bible reading

Matthew 1:19

There is not much written about Joseph in Luke's Gospel, except that he was from the house and line of David and was pledged to be married to Mary (Luke 2:4–5). So in order to delve deeper into who Joseph was and discover what his life teaches us, we are turning our attention to the Gospel of Matthew today.

Joseph was quite clearly a righteous man. Can you imagine discovering that your wife-to-be is pregnant, and yet knowing you are not the father? Mary shares the story with Joseph of the angel visiting her to tell her that she would give birth to the Son of the Most High God. He must have thought and questioned if he was marrying someone mentally unstable or, at the very least, an adulteress! And yet, Joseph does not expose her to public disgrace; he has in mind to 'divorce her quietly' (v19). He wanted to do the right thing and be faithful to the Law, even though it must have made him confused and angry. Joseph managed to think with a steady head, despite the series of events surrounding him.

However, we see that Joseph finds a way to do what it right in a way that is far more superior to the Law. He is obedient to the Lord of all the universe. Joseph does not divorce Mary but is visited by the angel and then does what the Lord commands him to do, 'take Mary home as your wife' (Matt. 1:20). Joseph is faithful and open to God, even waiting to consummate the marriage until after Jesus is born.

Sometimes we have a plan that seems right with the world, perhaps right with the law as well, but then God reveals a different way ahead. We cannot predict what God is going to do, nor must we limit Him with our rules and control; we need to stay open to His guiding hand. What Joseph thought was right to do before the angel came was different after his encounter. One of the biggest challenges in this passage is not being governed by what others will think or say or even do to you, but being led by the Spirit of God. Close friends and family must have questioned why Joseph was still going to marry an apparent 'adulteress' but he did it anyway. We must not let people lead us. God is the only true guide.

Perhaps the Lord wants to change some of our thinking. Both Zechariah and Joseph remained faithful and obedient to the Lord, but their view of who He was, what He could do and how much He cared for them changed radically. When we encounter the Lord we are never the same again.

Ponder
2 Corinthians 3:18; Romans 12:2; Philippians 3:21

Questions to consider
- Have you encountered Christ recently?
- Have you ever experienced the Lord change your plans?
- What happened?
- Do you remain faithful in worship and obedience to the Lord?

Reflect
Read and consider the words in Psalm 1.

DAY 12

Expect the unexpected

Opening prayer

Awesome God, thank You for Your creativity and that You are so much bigger and more incredible than our human minds can comprehend. Thank You that Your ways are not our ways. Help us live like You. Amen.

Bible reading

Matthew 1:21–23

Joseph was a man who lived by the Law, who followed Jewish rules and degrees and sought to honour the Lord with his whole life. This did not go unseen by God – he chose Joseph not only because he was from the line of David, but because he was also an upright man after God's heart. Joseph must have been shocked when he learnt who the Lord truly was and what He expected from him. I think that, after encountering the angel and watching what unfolded, Joseph's intimacy and realisation of His Father's love for him must have been so much deeper and stronger.

Sometimes we are in danger of assuming we know what is best for us, of thinking that our plan, our way, is the only way that we will consider. Some of us don't like surprises and would rather follow a faith of order. The truth is that we just have to look at the creation narrative to know that, in fact, the Lord likes things laid out and done well – including resting on the seventh day! He is not a chaotic God, He is creative and consistent.

What I love, however, about the story of Jesus coming into the world is that it is not as we predict, not in a way that we expect nor at a time that we would have set aside. Joseph had no idea that the angel would appear on that day at that time. Our God is in the business of doing incredible, unexpected things in moments that only He knows about. We cannot pin him down to our agenda or fit his plans and purposes in human boxes. The Lord will move by His Spirit as and when He chooses.

I love the thought that if God can take away something you've never expected losing, He can replace it with something that you've never imagined having. Although Joseph was not a biological father to Jesus, he was the human father of the Son of God!

When my family and I left the West Midlands to head for London due to job changes, I left behind a lot of local friendships and a very settled, established life. At the time it was really hard to understand why I had to leave a comfortable home, where the children were so settled, and venture out on an unknown path – but I knew God was calling us. We ended up moving locations very quickly but we have seen God's great faithfulness in our lives. I have gained more time to spend with my husband, great new friends, a new church, new job and so much more. This happened because we said 'yes' to God. If we can expect the unexpected with the Lord, we will be open to so much more. Be prepared to let Him surprise you!

Ponder
Romans 11:33–36

Questions to consider
- Are you open to the unexpected?
- Have you ever lost something but then gained something more?
- What did that do to your faith in God?

Reflect
Read or say aloud Psalm 139:1–12 (particularly note verse 8 – the Lord is with you wherever you go).

DAY 13

An unusual setting

Opening prayer

King of kings, thank You so much for humbling Yourself and becoming a servant. Thank You that Your love reaches to the least and lowliest place. Please help me to model a life like Yours. Amen.

Bible reading

Luke 1:26; Matthew 1:24–25

I wonder what the Jews imagined when they thought of their Messiah coming. When they looked at the prophetic voices in their past, did they begin to dream that He would make an appearance in their life time? Perhaps they thought the King of the world would be born in Jerusalem, that was the most obvious place after all – it was the prestigious centre of Jewish life and worship. And yet, when the King comes to earth it is not in a way that any of us would ever predict or imagine. Again, God's ways are not our ways. Joseph and Mary are in Nazareth, a small, poor town, miles away from Jerusalem. The human father of Jesus is a carpenter, earning little and living in a place of little importance or significance. The Lord God of heaven and earth takes up residence in a lowly place – not the highest place on earth but one of poverty and humility.

The beginning of Jesus' life is vitally important to our understanding of the kingdom and being His followers. Our Lord did not choose to arrive in a palace or a place of greatness and authority because He wanted to show us that He comes into the most unusual, poorest, weakest, despised places. Jesus comes to take the lowest to the highest place. He is not interested in our rank or position in life, nor is He interested in what the world thinks of us, He does not care how much money we have or how well-known we are – no, Jesus looks at our hearts.

When the Lord looked at Joseph, He saw a man who loved Him and followed Him faithfully – these were the things that mattered to Him. I wonder if Joseph sat down after the visit from the angel and thought 'why me?'. Maybe he questioned his position and occupation and how he could be the man for the job, or perhaps he just knew that none of that mattered.

The Bible is so clear that we must be prepared to serve, to come last, to humble ourselves (see Matt. 20:27; Luke 1:52; Luke 14:11; Gal. 5:13). We are called to live like Jesus did – not to exalt ourselves and seek position for human praise – but to have an attitude like Christ by making ourselves 'nothing, and taking the very nature of a servant' (Phil. 2:7–9). This is so challenging because it is not a call to live an oppressed life where we do not stand up for truth and righteousness; nor is it a call to hold back from doing all that we can with what God has given us. No, the key is to become more like Christ and therefore doing all that we do for Him and knowing that He does it through us. It is all about and all for Jesus, not for our own fame and recognition.

Ponder
Philippians 2:1–13 (particularly verse 13)

Questions to consider
- Why do you think the Lord chose Joseph to be Jesus' human father instead of a rich man in Jerusalem?
- Have you known the Lord move in an unusual setting or through a person that surprised you?
- Are you prepared to take the place of lowest honour?

Reflect
Meditate on 2 Chronicles 34:27 and consider: do you humble yourself?

DAY 14

Listen to the Lord

Opening prayer

Lord, thank You for the way that Simeon heard You leading and guiding him. Thank You for the ability to wait for You. Please help me to be patient and to follow Your lead more. Amen.

Bible reading

Luke 2:25–35

Today's reading has to be one of the best bits in the whole of Scripture! Here we are introduced to an incredible man and the reason that we love him is not because he is an old, wise man or that he gets to hold Jesus in his arms – no, he is an amazing example of one who really knows the Lord. He clearly has a deep and beautiful relationship with God where he is able to hear what the Spirit is saying. Verse 26 says, 'It had been revealed to him by the Holy Spirit that he would not die before he had seen the Lord's Messiah' – wow, imagine hearing the Spirit saying something as incredible as that! We also know that he didn't just hear the Lord speak to him once, but in the next verse we realise that Simeon's life was governed by God's leading hand; 'Moved by the Spirit, he went into the temple courts' (v27). Here is a man who listens to the Lord and is so devout that his entire life is led by the Holy Spirit.

This is before Jesus ascends into heaven. This is before He sends the Holy Spirit to the disciples at the beginning of Acts. Throughout Scripture, the Spirit is at work in powerful ways, revealing the heart of God to those who press into Him and seek His face. Simeon's heart cry is to know the Lord more than anything else. He is waiting for the consolation of Israel – he knows his Scripture and the Spirit has revealed to him some of the purpose for Christ's life (vv34–35).

I was listening to a speaker recently who, when she had finished, did not rush straight away into a prayer time, keen to get to the coffee break; she stopped, waited and listened to the Lord. She did not mind that there were over 1,500 people watching her and expecting her to speak; instead she prioritised listening to the Lord. After what seemed like forever, but was probably only about five minutes, she called someone out of the crowd whom she believed God wanted to heal – one person with a blood condition who didn't know Jesus. That afternoon we witnessed the Spirit of God come and heal but also lead a loved one into a relationship with Christ. It was awesome.

This speaker showed me that listening to the Spirit of God is the most important thing we can do, wherever we are and whatever we are doing. We can go the world's way, or we can go God's way. Simeon's story and life are not there like an ornament to marvel at and say, 'well that is what the children of God used to be like', he is there to remind us to push into listening to God and to expect the Spirit to move in power today. Our concern is giving Him the space to do just that!

Ponder
Psalm 5:3; Micah 7:7; Isaiah 30:18

Questions to consider
- Do you have a space to listen and wait for the Lord?
- Are you hungry to hear His voice and be led by Him more?
- When was the last time that you felt 'moved by the Spirit'?

Reflect
In response to the questions above, turn your thoughts into prayers.

DAY 15

Hold on to His promises

Opening prayer

Lord, thank You for Simeon's life. Thank You that he was willing to wait and that he saw his longings answered. Please help us, Father, to wait patiently for You and hold on to Your promises. Amen.

Bible reading

Luke 2:25,29–32

Reading the short account of Simeon's encounter with Christ, there is one word that sticks out of the passage so strongly. It is not written in bold in the Bible, but I think it should be, 'Simeon was *waiting* for the consolation of Israel' (v25, my emphasis). Simeon knew that he was going to see the Messiah but he had no idea when, how or what that would look like. He was waiting patiently and faithfully for the Lord's promise to be fulfilled. A couple of verses later, Simeon says to the Lord, 'Sovereign Lord, as you have promised, you now dismiss your servant in peace' (v29). The wait is over and the peace of the Lord has come to Simeon.

I don't know what you are waiting for at the moment or what you feel that the Lord has promised to you, but Simeon is an incredible example of a man who holds on to God's promise and is willing to wait for Him to fulfil it. We live in such an instant society, where we can have whatever we want at the click of a button, never mind going out to get it from a shop. If we want to visit someone, we have many options of transport we can use to get to them. If we want to communicate with people we can contact them in numerous ways using many forms of technology, whenever we want to. We can make lots of things happen in our lives, very quickly, without waiting for them. Consider standing in a queue in the supermarket, waiting for our turn at the till – many of us are likely constantly checking to see if another line is shorter and asking ourselves if it would be better to switch lanes to get through faster! In fact, when we find that we do have to wait, we can get very impatient – we feel frustrated and there is a sense that we 'should have it sooner' or it 'should be sorted by now'. We may have plenty of time but we are still looking for the quickest way to get the outcome that we want. No wonder so many of us struggle with stress!

If Simeon was living today I wonder if he would search online for the Messiah or try and get the number in order to call Mary and Joseph? Perhaps he would jump in his car or get on the train and go looking for him so that he could see the consolation of Israel sooner!

Interestingly, life was not like that for Simeon, so he had to wait and pray, but it did not mean that he had to give up because he fervently believed God's plans would be fulfilled. It is challenging because I wonder how often we should be waiting and praying, rather than trying to fix everything in our own time.

The very idea of waiting and holding onto God's promises, without taking action, is uncomfortable and challenging for most of us. Perhaps it is time to practise waiting.

Ponder
Isaiah 40:27–31

Questions to consider
• What are you waiting for?
• Is it time to stop trying to make something happen and wait for the Lord to move?

Reflect
Read Micah 7:7 and declare the reading as a decision over your life today.

THREE

Seek Him first

Luke 2:8–20,36–38; Matthew 2:1-16

DAY 16

Deep intimacy

Opening prayer

Lord, thank You for revealing Yourself and Your plans to Anna.
Thank You for her example of intimacy with You. Help us, Father, to
find ways to deepen our intimacy with You. Amen.

Bible reading

Luke 2:36–38

When you read about Anna you cannot help but think of a nun or a
monk – someone who has committed their whole life, all their waking
and sleeping, to God. I don't know what you think about nuns or
monks but I think it is fair to say that most of us would consider them
to be very holy people, no doubt because they spend so much time
focused on the Lord. Anna 'never left the temple but worshipped night
and day, fasting and praying' (v37); constantly spending time in the
Lord's house, her whole world was at His feet. She was without doubt
a very holy lady, with a heart totally devoted to God.

We could argue that being in the Temple night and day was a bit
unhelpful to the rest of the world around her. Just as a monk is tucked
away in a monastery, we might wonder if the Lord would long for them
to be sharing the truth of who He is in their local communities. However,
who are we to judge? Anna clearly had a 'direct line' to the Lord as she
knew about the promised child and the redemption of Jerusalem. What if
this one conversation with Joseph, Mary and Jesus, was the one that the
Lord had been preparing her for – a moment in her life ordained by the
King. I am sure it was!

We can be doing, serving and trying to change situations around us
without knowing who we are doing it for. Our lives can get so busy
and 'important' that the idea of worshipping night and day seems like

a lazy or unnecessary part of our journey. The truth is that I envy Anna's deep intimacy with the Lord. I know I cannot spend all my time physically on my knees in the Temple (I mean, think of the leg pain!) but I want to know Him like she did.

God revealed great things to Anna because He knew that she loved Him and sought His face above all else. God knew that He came first in Anna's life. Now I know we don't necessarily have lives like Anna's but we do have access to the Lord. He has torn down the dividing wall of hostility and made a way for us. We do not need permission to enter the Holy of Holies, Jesus has opened up the way. We do not need to go to the Temple every day; we can worship the Lord wherever we are. We can spend time with the Lord all the time, involving Him in all that we do and every decision we make.

Even if we carry lots of responsibility, we can still have intimacy with Christ. The question is: are we going to seek this intimacy with Him? It does not mean we stop serving and sharing who He is, but that we are led more clearly by His agenda, not our own.

Ponder
Genesis 12:1–9

Questions to consider
- How would you feel about following the Lord, over and above your own plans?
- Do you long for the kind of intimacy Anna had? Why not share your heart with the Lord?

Reflect
Pray the words of Psalm 25:5 and think about what they may mean to you.

DAY 17

Respecting our elders

Opening prayer

*Lord Jesus, thank You that You use us at whatever age and stage
we are at in our life. Please help us to honour and respect our
elders in the way that You would. Amen.*

Bible reading

Luke 2:36–37

One of the most beautiful qualities that I have observed in my Nigerian
friends is the utmost respect they have for those older than themselves.
When an older lady tries to help them in the kitchen, they encourage
her to sit down and they look after her needs. Even more than that,
they don't make an older person feel useless, they seek wisdom and
advice from them in regard to everything that they do. If they are
cooking a meal, they would ask their elders how to do it. When they
are raising their children, they seek advice from their parents and
'aunties'. The younger generations do not assume to know better
than those who have gone before. I know that this respect for elders
is common in other cultures too, but for some reason it has spoken
particularly poignantly to me recently.

I think in our Western culture we can be in danger of making the
older generations feel like they are past their sell by date or that they
have nothing of value to offer. Once someone has got a bit older and
has begun to slow down in what they are able to do, we can sometimes
stop valuing them. I sometimes wonder whether the Lord wants us to
open our eyes to the generations that have gone before – not looking to
them to do what they used to do, but to enlist their help in other ways.
The truth is that wisdom grows in us as we get older and we need to
share that wisdom. Perhaps, instead of looking to the older folk to make

the tea at church, we might choose to sit down and ask their advice on something. Maybe if we blessed them with a meal, we could allow them to bless us with a prayer or a listening ear.

Anna was eighty-four years old when she spoke prophetically over Jesus. She was an incredibly wise old lady who knew the Lord so intimately. In today's society it's possible that we could overlook such a person, passing them by on the street as an old vulnerable human being – and yet Anna was a powerful tool in the hand of God.

We have a few of these power tools in their eighties at my church, and boy, are they a gift from the Lord! When they pray the atmosphere changes, when they speak we stop and slow our decisions down – they remind us that God is not in a rush and His wisdom needs to be revealed. I love the fact that Anna was older because it is a reminder that age does not limit who or what we do for Jesus. I am often challenged to look at the older folk differently and treat them with the respect that my Nigerian friends have shown. After all, the Lord made it clear that we are His body here on earth, whatever our age, colour, or background, and we are challenged to value every part of the body equally.

Ponder
Leviticus 19:32; 1 Timothy 5:1–7; Ephesians 6:1–3

Questions to consider
- Who are the older people in your life?
- Do you show respect and care towards them?
- Is there something you can do to show your respect for your elders this week, even if it is simply to smile when you next see them?

Reflect
Read Proverbs 4, asking the Lord to increase your wisdom.

DAY 18

A big picture

Opening prayer

Glorious Father, thank You for the image in our minds of Your light and glory coming to that hillside on that memorable night. Thank You that You brought good news for all of us. Please help us to understand more of what You have saved us from and why You have come to us. Amen.

Bible reading

Luke 2:8–9

There are an incredible series of revelations throughout Scripture regarding the Messiah. Here, in Luke 2, we read about a group of shepherds up on the hillside who are visited by a group of angels. Mary and Joseph had no idea that anyone else was finding out their secret; they thought it was just happening where they were. However, the Lord was at work within a much bigger picture – drawing others to worship Him, which is why He comes to the shepherds. A bit like Mary and Joseph in a little, unknown town, the angels come to unexpected and lowly people. And once again, we are reminded that our Lord does not choose to work in the highest place to proclaim the arrival of Christ – He heads to the hillside.

As always an even bigger picture is at work here, bigger than Nazareth and Bethlehem, bigger than all the people involved right there and then in the story; these shepherds may have been the very ones providing the lambs for the sacrifices in the Temple; lambs slain for the forgiveness of human sin. Here, the angels are revealing to these men that the ultimate Lamb has been born in a stable – a perfect spotless Saviour – born to remove the sins of the entire world, forever.

I wonder what the shepherds made of this angelic greeting on the hillside. Being used to working in all weathers, in the dark, I bet it took a lot to frighten them and yet we read that they were afraid. Their fear quickly turns to joy though, as they hear the words spoken and the praises sung. The light and sound must have been more amazing than anything we could imagine! The shepherds were merely men taking care of their sheep, yet the angels came to them in such a magnificent way!

The Lord wants to come to us too, whoever we are, whatever we think of ourselves and whatever we have done. He has a plan for our lives that is far more exciting than we could dream or understand. He wants to wipe our slate clean again, inviting us to be cleansed by His blood, so that we can know Him more. The Lord did not want the shepherds to keep offering lambs as a sacrifice for sin forever, He wanted them to understand that the Lamb of God (John 1:36) had arrived, the Lamb who would deal with their sin and ours once and for all.

Ponder
Isaiah 7:14 – God at work in an even bigger picture

Questions to consider
- Do you believe that God wants to come to you?
- Have you thought about the reality of this baby as the Saviour for all the world?
- Jesus comes to you, to me and to the whole world, to save us from death. Why not invite Him to show you what this salvation mean for you?

Reflect
Allow the words of Psalm 119:41 and Matthew 11:28 to minister to you.

DAY 19

Don't compare

Opening prayer

Lord, thank You for coming to the hepherds, and thank You that You want to come to me too. Please help me not to compare myself with others, but to see myself as You see me. Amen.

Bible reading

Luke 2:10–12

The angel says to the shepherds 'I bring you good news of great joy that will cause great joy for all the people' (v10). The angel doesn't say 'I am on my way to the magi to tell them this message of hope, which I will just quickly share with you too, as I am passing'. Scripture reveals something so important here. The news of Jesus' birth was shared with shepherds, who usually would have thought themselves nothing in comparison to the magi or the priests at the Temple. The message is clear – the good news is for *all* people.

We don't just see wealthy, wise magi discovering through their studies that the King has been born. We see poor, uneducated shepherds encountering Christ too. Sometimes we can be in danger of looking at other people, and think that they are better than us, that they have greater understanding of Christ because they are intelligent or because they are ordained. There is a human failing in us that compares who we are and what we have achieved with those who appear 'better' than us.

The enemy takes this tendency to compare and uses it to crush our confidence, our sense of belonging and to question our belief that God values who we are. We can feel like a lowly shepherd on a hillside with an empty life – perhaps feeling invisible and worthless. We might try and compete with those that we believe are worth more in the eyes of God.

And yet the angel says to the shepherds, 'I bring *you* good news' (v10). He says to Mary; '*you* are highly favoured' (Luke 1:28, both my emphasis). We need to take hold of these words: Christ comes to *us*, to *you*, with His good news and it is because *you* are favoured, He loves *you*. Whatever we think of ourselves, we can know Christ is in us and with us. His love is not limited to what we can do or how we may look or how much we earn. The world may value wealth, prosperity and appearance, but these things are not high on the Lord's agenda.

Looking to the right or the left and comparing ourselves to siblings, colleagues, neighbours or Christian brothers and sisters will only take our eyes off what Christ wants to do through us and more importantly, how He sees us. Max Lucado has written a great children's book entitled *You are Special* and in it he notes the comparisons that we make and how they make us feel worthless. However, as we get to know our Maker, we realise that 'all that matters is what He thinks and He thinks we are really special'.* Spending time with Jesus helps us to stop comparing ourselves to others as we realise how deeply special we are to Him – just as we are. Jesus calls us to fix our eyes on Him; 'The pioneer and perfecter of our faith' (Heb. 12:2), seeking intimacy with Him. The more that we understand the Lord's love for us, the less we compare ourselves to others: we begin to see who we are through the Father's eyes.

Ponder

Exodus 4:1–18

Questions to consider

- Do you struggle with comparison?
- Who do you compare yourself to and why?
- How is it affecting how you see yourself?

Reflect

Read John 3:16, asking the Lord to speak to you in a new way.

*Max Lucado, *You are Special* (Candle Books, 2004), p25

An urgent message

Opening prayer

Lord Jesus, thank You for the urgency and joy that the shepherds felt at the thought of sharing Your message. Please help me to recognise the good news afresh and be hungry to share it with others. Amen.

Bible reading

Luke 2:17–20

The response of the shepherds is absolutely amazing. After the angels leave them, they do not return quietly to the hillside, instead they do the complete opposite! When they encounter the Lord, the shepherds do two really notable things. Firstly, they 'spread the word concerning what had been told them about this child' (v17) and secondly, they left, 'glorifying and praising God for all the things that they had heard and seen' (v20).

The shepherds could have run off to tell their friends about the visit from the angel, not waiting until they had seen the Messiah – in essence, they could have told them only half of the story. The shepherds could have chosen to stay quiet on the hillside, out of fear of what might happen if they began proclaiming that a Saviour was born. They might have been too tired to praise God or spread the word. These men might have decided to keep the information to themselves and not see the value of sharing it.

And yet, we witness the shepherds immediately sharing the good news that they have seen the Saviour. They could not keep it a secret, they were overwhelmed with joy by what they had seen in the stable and their encounter on the hills! The shepherds knew that the story had to be told, and it had to be told straight away. Something inside them welled up to such a point that all they could do was glorify and praise the Lord's name. A new chapter, a new life had begun for them and for all people. The angel isn't recorded as telling the shepherds specifically to tell the world about the new Messiah and I am pretty sure Mary and Joseph didn't either – they had enough to think about! However, the shepherds just could not stay silent!

It makes me think about when someone gets engaged – they are desperate to tell people the good news. Equally when you or a loved one falls pregnant, it is almost impossible not to let the delight spill from your lips. Good news brings great joy and when you know it is for 'all the people', not just your friends and family, how can you possibly keep it to yourself?

I wonder how many of us feel like the shepherds this Advent, carrying an urgent message that we are desperate to share? Is joy bubbling up inside us so much that we are glorifying and praising God? The shepherds hurried off to see the baby Jesus – are we longing to see Him too?

Ponder
John 4:1–42 (particularly focusing on verses 27–30,39–42)

Questions to consider
- Can you take a few moments to praise God for Christ's life, death and resurrection?
- Is the central Advent truth of Jesus, good news to you?
- Who are you sharing Christ with this Christmas?
- Maybe it's time to pray for a sense of urgency to share His message and for a new joy to well up inside you?

Reflect
Read Acts 4:8–12, considering and asking for Peter's sense of urgency to share the truth of the gospel.

DAY 21

Do you want to see Jesus?

Opening prayer

Lord Jesus, the magi were faithful to You, seeking Your face above everything else. Please help me to seek more of You and spend more time with You. Amen.

Bible reading

Matthew 2:1–12

Delving into the magi narrative is very exciting. Realising that there were a group of wise men (we are unsure of exactly how many) who travelled thousands of miles to see King Jesus. These men dedicated their lives to finding this Saviour who was going to be born. The wise men would have studied their history notes in depth, for years questioning the time and place of the arrival of the Messiah. They may well have been influenced by words like those in Numbers 24:17: 'I see him, but not now; I behold him, but not near. A star will come out of Jacob; a sceptre will rise out of Israel.' It could have been words like these (even though uttered by Balaam, who was a sorcerer!) that convinced the men to travel towards Israel.

It's amazing to picture these wise men studying texts and then making the decision to leave their homeland and to travel into the unknown. The idea that a group of men would choose to look for Jesus, over and above everything else in their lives, not knowing what would happen, where they would end up or if they would even find Him, is incredible. The magi show us that looking for Jesus can and should be the highest priority in our lives.

It makes me wonder, what risks will we take to encounter Christ? Are we prepared to get out of our comfort zones and to travel to other places or speak to new people? We have two new team members from America soon joining our leadership team at church. Along with their two young children, they are leaving all their friends and family, secure jobs, everything that is familiar to them, to begin a new life here in north London. Why are they doing it? Because they believe that the Lord is calling them to be part of the work here. As a family, they want to see Jesus move in power and join in with what He is doing in this neighbourhood.

People no doubt believed that the magi were crazy to set off on such an unknown journey but their hunger and desire to see the Saviour was a driver in their hearts that could not be ignored. The family who are joining our leadership team have a similar desire – they want to follow God with everything and they trust that He will make a way for them, just as He did for the wise men thousands of years ago. The question for us all as we head towards Christmas is – are we prioritising looking for Him over and above everything else in our lives? This may not necessarily mean travelling east, but making subtle changes to your daily plans.

Ponder
Acts 9:10–19

Questions to consider
• Do you want to see Jesus?
• Is there somewhere He wants you to go something He wants you to or do for Him?

Reflect
Read Matthew 5:1–12, asking the Lord, 'Which one am I?'

DAY 22

Where are you looking for Jesus?

Opening prayer

Father, thank You that the magi did not stop looking for You when they got to the palace. Thank You that they went on to Bethlehem. Lord, help me to find You and not get side-tracked by this world. Amen.

Bible reading

Matthew 2:1–6

The magi journey from the East, not to Bethlehem where Jesus was born, but to Jerusalem – the obvious place to look for a king – in a palace! They go to King Herod and ask him, 'Where is the one who has been born king of the Jews? We saw his star when it rose and have come to worship him' (v2). Why wouldn't you go to the palace to look for a baby king? You would hardly put a shanty town in the sat nav if you were trying to locate Prince George!

It is interesting that the magi's journey led them to the palace – a place of wealth and royalty, a destination of human power and authority, the pinnacle of society and the ultimate seat of control – and yet our journey with Christ leads us to the opposite place – it leads us to the cross. When we encounter Jesus, we don't find ourselves in a place of human gain but in a place of surrender. Meeting the King of the world is not about receiving human riches but eternal ones.

Following their encounter with King Herod, thankfully, the journey of the magi was not over and the Lord set them back on the right track towards Bethlehem. But it raises the question, 'Where is our journey taking us?'

If we are honest with ourselves we may find that our priorities are wrong. For example, so often life can be about us finding a good house in a nice area with good schools and great friends. Our focus can be on the latest furniture catalogue or online bargains and yet, what are we trying to achieve? Where are we intending to go? As Isaiah reminds us, 'The grass withers and the flowers fall, but only the word of our God endures forever' (Isa. 40:8). We can put all our trust in reaching the palace, in creating a human paradise, and yet these things will pass away. God calls us to take a different journey, to a stable and ultimately to a cross; being willing to lay down our own map and to take a look at a new route. A journey with Jesus is not straightforward, nor will it tick all the boxes that we had imagined, but it is the most fulfilling way to go and it will last for eternity.

On a visit once to see the way that the Amish people live, I was challenged by a sign above an Amish family's doorway. Instead of the usual 'GOD BLESS AMERICA' that I had become used to seeing in so many places, their slogan read, 'AMERICA BLESS GOD'. Instead of looking for the Lord to bless us and meet all our needs, we need to ask the Lord to help us to shift our direction, seeking to bless Him first.

Ponder
Psalm 146 (particularly verse 3)

Questions to consider
- Are you looking for Jesus in the right place?
- Has your journey stopped at the palace – in a place of comfort and wealth?
- Is the Lord calling you to look for Him somewhere else?

Reflect
Look at Isaiah 40:8 and consider if you are building for eternity.

Mistakes don't signal the end

Opening prayer

Almighty God, thank You for Your forgiveness. Thank You that mistakes don't signal the end and that we can begin again. Please help us to get back on the right road with You, just like the magi did. Amen.

Bible reading

Matthew 2:10–16

When we picture the magi following the star and arriving at the stable, we imagine a striking, joyful scene. Smartly dressed gentlemen arrive in a cattle shed, they bow down and offer gifts to the new-born King and worship Him. For many of us telling the nativity story, we stop the narrative there, especially if we are sharing it with children, because the next bit is a difficult pill to swallow – Herod orders his army to kill all the little boys under two years old in Bethlehem.

The magi may have found out from Herod's men that they should head to Bethlehem (Matt. 2:5), but their trip to the palace also had horrific consequences. The magi made a huge mistake sharing timings and information with Herod (Matt. 2:2,16) and because they did not return to the palace, Herod ordered a mass killing of all the baby boys in the area. There was a huge cost to this trip from the East – yes, the wise men saw Jesus and worshipped Him; yes, their journey eventually led them to the right place; however, there was a major mistake along the way that might have been avoided.

Thankfully, the Lord led the wise men back to their country by another route (v12). Our Lord and Father was gracious to the men, and their mistake did not cause them to lose their lives.

We can set off on a journey through life, longing to see Jesus, to worship Him and to serve Him with our whole lives but we all make mistakes along the way. The truth is that the death and resurrection of Jesus Christ means that we can begin again, we can set course for a new destination. We can pray over the mistakes that we have made and ask God to have mercy on us and on those that have been affected by our wrong actions.

The story of the magi is incredible because, together, they reveal lives that are completely dedicated to seeking Christ. However, their journey also serves as an encouragement to us that, at times, the children of God do mess up, even if they feel that they are being guided correctly and trying to do the right thing – we know that there is grace and forgiveness for us at the cross if we have gone down a blind alley. Finally, the magi serve as a warning to us to listen carefully for the Lord's leading, to wait and not assume we know best, to expect the unexpected and to get back on course as quick as we can.

The magi's mistake was costly but it did not signal the end of the story.

Ponder
James 1:1–12

Questions to consider
• Have you ever made a mistake like the magi did?
• Is it time to get back on the right road again?
• Why not pray for those affected by your actions? Know that the Lord can wipe anyone's slate clean.

Reflect
Read Jeremiah 31:1–6, reminding yourself that God's desire is to rebuild our lives.

FOUR

Who will you live for?

Matthew 25; Luke 1:1-4,32; 2:10,30-35

DAY 24

Examine our motives

Opening prayer

Lord, I love You and I know that I am a sinner in need of a Saviour. Please examine my heart and mind and help me not to respond in a way that will cause hurt and pain to others. Amen.

Bible reading

Matthew 2:3,7

Scripture often uses one or two words to reveal so much to us. When we consider Herod, his actions reveal that he was a king who ruled in a terrible way. However, Scripture also helps us learn things about Herod's character, the man behind the decisions, which helps us to consider what makes us 'go wrong' in our own lives. We read in verse 3 of chapter 2 that when Herod heard the news of a new king arriving, he was 'disturbed', and all Jerusalem with him. What does this tell us about Herod? The news of a new king rattled him to his very core; his normal pattern of life was shaken, which means that he would not have behaved 'normally' after receiving this news. Jerusalem (his people) were disturbed too, and Herod would have known this. In this situation the king has to 'do something' – in his mind action would have to be taken. It is then that we see a clear moment of deception and dishonesty, as he calls the magi 'secretly' and convinces them to go to Bethlehem and then report back, so that he can 'worship' Jesus too (vv7–8).

The challenge here is that Herod's feelings lead to what seems to be good and honest behaviour, but there are evil, underlying motives at work, which ultimately lead to him ordering the killing of baby boys. Our feelings can be very powerful and have the potential to lead us into acting in horrendous ways – even if we believe that we started the journey with the right intentions. Whether we feel competitive or insecure as a result of a situation we find ourselves in – our feelings can lead us into doing and saying things that are ungodly. It may seem as though there are other people that feel the same as us, and therefore there seems to be greater pressure to act; in those situations we need even more prayer for discernment! Whether we are furious (Matt. 2:16) or disturbed (v3), we have a choice in how we manage those feelings.

When I was at college, one of my lecturers said, 'Little tigers grow into big tigers and big tigers kill'. It challenged me to consider my motives, examine my heart and be more careful in making decisions. Herod's narrative is a very helpful wake-up call and causes us to think about our behaviour. When I stand chatting in the school playground, listening to the latest gossip, I have a choice – do I join in with the crowd and add my comments, perhaps making assumptions in my mind about the teachers, the school or other parents, or do I say something positive and walk away? Every day we hear unhealthy news and we have a choice as to how we respond. We also have a choice whether to let our feelings dictate our behaviour or instead ask the Lord to fill us with His compassion and understanding. The more we do the latter, the more we can walk in step with Christ.

Ponder
Galatians 5:13–26

Questions to consider
• Are your feelings dictating your behaviour?
• Why not ask the Lord to give you His Spirit's strength to act as He would?

Reflect
Read Psalm 26 aloud and ask the Lord to help you to keep standing on level ground.

DAY 25

Be authentic

Opening prayer

Lord, we thank You for the scriptural example of Herod and what he teaches us. Please help us to build our lives on Your rock and be authentic disciples who truly belong to You. Amen.

Bible reading

Matthew 2:8

Herod is a fascinating character in the Bible. In this king we see both a builder and a destroyer. He was a man who built great structures, a huge empire, and yet he was also a man who destroyed many peoples' lives. Herod even went as far as killing some of his own family – including a few of his children – his behaviour was twisted and evil.

This builder and destroyer shows us something really interesting: we can build great things – impressive structures, businesses, churches and homes – but what are we like towards people? We can have all the appearance of being someone truly great and yet inside we are far from loving towards God and one another. If we only work on the external part of our lives, the inside will crash and burn. There is a real challenge to us as children of God to be those who honour the Lord in public and in private. Are we people who are building a public façade that is different to the person we are at home?

Herod's empire was impressive and yet thoroughly broken. He was not building on the Rock, he was building on sand. He was using human power, fear and manipulation to bring about a mighty earthly kingdom, whilst his character became more and more twisted as time went on. Some of us may have witnessed Christian leaders fall because of sin: something in their character influenced their behaviour in a way that led them to do what they probably never dreamt of doing. The truth is we are all sinners in need of a Saviour to impact every part of our lives.

Jesus tells His children to build on rock, to have a firm foundation in love, humility and peace. There seems to be a real call for us, as His disciples, to live lives that build up, not tear down. I believe He longs for us to live authentically and be true to following Christ in private as well as in public. The authentic followers of the Lord are those who are committed to loving Him no matter what and loving others with everything that we are. This is about encouraging, caring, putting others before ourselves and sacrificing.

Herod was building an earthly kingdom but he was destroying people's lives. In contrast Jesus calls us to build for an eternal kingdom and encourage as many as we can to come on that journey too, through love and prayer. The question is, are we being authentic? Is what we are building in public the same as what we are doing in private? What makes the world happy is not the same as what brings a smile to the face of Christ.

Ponder
Matthew 7:21–29

Questions to consider
- What are you building your life on?
- Are you building something that will fall apart or last forever?
- Do you behave differently in public to how you behave in private?
- Perhaps it's time to ask God to help you to live more authentically?

Reflect
Read 2 Corinthians 4:7–12, asking God to help you live for Him in everything.

DAY 26

Act out of love

Opening prayer

Father, please reveal more of Your love to us so that it runs deeper into our hearts, rolling out to affect the lives of those we love and the people around us. Amen.

Bible reading

Matthew 2:16–18

I sometimes wonder how many of my actions are motivated by love – by Christ's deep, selfless, unconditional love. When we accept Jesus into our hearts, He comes and helps us live lives that express His love to the rest of the world. I don't know about you but there are moments, days and even seasons when it can feel like I am not acting in a very loving way.

When I think about waking each day, getting the kids up, dressed, breakfasted, organised and out of the door for school, I do not think I am very loving! In fact I am often frustrated, impatient and tired! In these moments it can feel like any love that I have has gone cold. I am not looking after my little people with a soft heart, like I do when they are snuggled in their beds at night, but rather a cold, hard heart that I find hard to recognise.

As we have seen, Herod allowed his cold, hard heart to become so furious, so angry, so jealous and insecure, that he ordered the killing of all boys under the age of two in Bethlehem. His actions reveal a heart that was completely void of love. And yet, we know that the love of Christ can transform any heart.

If we are truly going to look different from our neighbours, if they are really going to encounter the love of Christ when they see us, then we need more of Him in us. We can become so familiar with the story: Jesus came to earth, he was born in a stable, suffered under Pontius

Pilate, was crucified, died and was buried. On the third day He rose again from the dead. He defeated the enemy, took all our sins upon Himself and enabled us to enter into relationship with Him. But do we forget, or even sometimes take for granted, the wonderful news that this relationship is unlike any other? Even though we know the story of what Jesus did for us, do we spend enough time with Him?

When Jesus is talking with the Jewish leaders He says, 'I know you. I know that you do not have the love of God in your hearts' (John 5:42). To Jesus, having this understanding of His love, transforms our lives and therefore we desperately need it! Not just 'head knowledge' but hearts that burn for Him.

Jesus longs to penetrate our human hearts with more of His love. He wants to meet with us and shatter the familiarity in our minds, by powerfully breaking through to our core. Many of us are good at knowing in our heads how to live rightly, but has the truth of the gospel touched our hearts? Do we really understand that Jesus loves us? I don't know about you, but I feel I need to know more of that unconditional love on a Monday morning!

Ponder
1 Corinthians 13:1–13; 16:14

Questions to consider
• Has your heart become hardened?
• Can you pinpoint moments when you struggled to love?
• Why not ask the Lord to reveal more of His love to you and to strengthen you to love others today?

Reflect
Consider what Christ has done for you on the cross. He did it because of His great love for you.

Who is Christ?

Opening prayer

Father, thank You that You didn't remain distant and set apart.
Thank You for sending Your Son into the world. We worship You
today! Amen.

Bible reading

Luke 1:32; 2:10

Over the next few days we will look afresh at what the prophets and
angels declared about Christ. Who was He? What did they proclaim
Him to be? It is so exciting to read these words and reflect on the
reality that they were being spoken before Jesus was born and then
over Him as a baby. The heavenly hosts and prophetic voices were
naming and proclaiming the truth of who Jesus was and would be!
We can read the words thinking, 'Yes, they were right! He most
certainly was and is all of those things.'

A friend of mine was telling me how a pastor was praying for him and
his wife, asking the Lord to give them a child. The church leader really
believed that He was being led to pray along these lines and that they
were going to have a baby. You could say this is dangerous territory and
it most certainly can be – however, his words were cautious and he was a
wise man. He uttered, 'I believe this is what the Lord might be saying, but
do not put all your faith in my words.' Nine months later, a baby boy was
born to the couple and 18 months after that, they took the child to visit
the pastor. He was overwhelmed with joy. He believed that the Lord was
going to provide them with a baby but it was still such a miracle to witness
the couple presenting the child and asking him to pray for them again.

The angel Gabriel doesn't just tell Mary that she is having a baby
but that He will be 'the Son of the Most High' (v32) – the Son of God!

How incredible! To be told that you are going to give birth to the Son of God! Later the angel of the Lord appears to the shepherds and says that this baby is good news and will bring great joy to all the people (2:9–10). These truths are being proclaimed ahead of the actual event taking place, and when we think of what happened afterwards we know with certainty that all of these words became a reality. The Son of the Most High came into the world for all of us with the best message ever, leaving us with a joy that outweighs any earthly happiness we could ever dream of.

It is so important to reflect on the fact that this wasn't just a normal baby, this was *the Son of God* who came to earth for us. During Advent we are reminded that the Lord did not remain distant and removed from the world, but gave up His glory to come and be born in the lowest place and live and die amongst us. He came because He loves you and me so much.

Ponder
Isaiah 53:1–12

Questions to consider
• Do you believe what the angels say, that Jesus is the Son of God?
• Is the message of Christ good news to you? Why?
• Have you experienced His joy? How has He changed your life?

Reflect
Read and declare John 1:49 a few times out loud to the Lord.

DAY 28

The Shepherd

Opening prayer

Lord Jesus, thank You that You are our Shepherd, constantly watching over and loving us. Please give us strength to walk through the valleys, to follow Your lead and to pray for those who are lost. Amen.

Bible reading

Matthew 2:6

There are so many incredible scriptures proclaiming who Jesus is and we are only able to cover a few of them in this study. We can understand just a tiny part of who He is and yet what we read is so diverse, beautiful and awesome. Imagine when we see Him face to face, how much more we will understand the depth of our Lord!

In today's prophecy, read by Herod's priests and teachers of the Law, we discover that Christ will be the Shepherd of Israel. This is a powerful image, especially knowing that Jesus is the perfect Lamb as well as the Shepherd of the flock. He becomes the least and lowest whilst without sin, and then Lord of all people, leading and guiding them for all eternity.

These words are fulfilled as we witness the life of Jesus throughout the Gospels. Jesus himself declares, 'I am the good shepherd. The good shepherd lays down his life for the sheep' (John 10:11). Again, in 1 Peter, as the good news begins to spread across the earth, it says, 'And when the Chief Shepherd appears, you will receive the crown of glory that will never fade away' (1 Pet. 5:4), 'For "you were like sheep going astray," but now you have returned to the Shepherd and Overseer of your souls' (1 Pet. 2:25).

The Shepherd of Israel becomes the Shepherd of all souls that are committed to the Lord Jesus Christ. When we think of Jesus as our Shepherd, we think of one who will not let any of us down, who will look for us and watch over us. He will guide us and protect us from the work of the evil one. He will never leave us – day or night. God never sleeps. Our Shepherd will work hard to lead us to green pastures, even though we may walk through valleys and across rivers. He will call for us and draw us near to Him and to others. The ultimate Shepherd is found in Jesus.

Perhaps you know someone today who is lost and you would love them to come back to Christ? Maybe there is someone in your family who lives far away or feels distant from the family and from faith in Jesus? Our God longs to draw them back. He cares for every single sheep and wants to include them in His fold. He does not want even one of them to be lost. The Lord Jesus will not force anyone to come to Him; He simply says, 'Here I am! I stand at the door and knock. If anyone hears my voice and opens the door, I will come in and eat with that person, and they with me' (Rev. 3:20).

Ponder
Jeremiah 31:10–14

Questions to consider
- Do you know Christ as your Shepherd?
- Are there areas of your life where you need His guidance and leading? Perhaps you need to know that He is watching over you.
- Why not ask the Lord to draw your friend or relative back to the rest of the flock today?

Reflect
Read John 10:9 and pray that those who are lost will find their way to the Gate to discover the Good Shepherd.

DAY 29

The Light of Revelation

Opening prayer

King of kings , thank You for saving me and revealing to us that You are truly the Saviour of the world. Thank You that Your message is for all of us. Please help me to pray that You will lift the veil from the hearts and minds of people I know. Amen.

Bible reading

Luke 2:32,35

The living Christ continues to reveal good news to us all! Jesus did not come purely to lead and shepherd the Israelites; He wanted to be a revelation for all people until the end of time.

When I was a little girl, I remember eagerly showing my mum a picture of a pink fairy castle cake that I had discovered in one of her crumpled food magazines. I begged her desperately to make the cake for my birthday party. I can picture her face now – slight terror, coupled with a sense of 'yes, I can master that'. On the day of my party I was so excited to see the cake! Mum had kept it hidden for a day or so and I couldn't wait for my friends to see what she had made. I knew it would be incredible and I would feel so proud of my mum. The 'Happy Birthday' song began, the lights were dimmed, and the lighted cake approached me at the table. When I had furiously blown out all the candles, I gazed down on the most fabulous fairy castle I had ever seen (so much better than in the magazine)! It filled me with joy to hear the gasps of 'wow' and 'can we try it?' fill the air. Mum had done it again – she had revealed something spectacular, and real, that I would never forget.

The coming Messiah was written and prophesied about. Those who studied the texts thought they had an idea of who He might be and what He would do for the Jews, but the reality was quite different. When

the Light of Revelation came, He uncovered a message so incredible –
He had not come just to save the Jews, but the Gentiles too. Jesus was
going to unveil hearts and minds, saving souls for eternity. The Christ
that they encountered was, like the birthday cake laid before me, a
million times more amazing than how they had imagined Him to be.

'But whenever anyone turns to the Lord, the veil is taken away'
(2 Cor. 3:16). In Christ the old veil, the old covenant, is removed and
the new one has come. The revelation in Jesus enables us to see and
understand and hear and be whole. We no longer encounter a far
off God whom we approach in a tent of meeting; the dividing wall
has been broken down and we can enter into a personal and loving
relationship with the Lord! This relationship can be known in a deep,
intimate way all the time. Those who don't know Christ sadly remain
with a veil over their hearts and minds, unable to hear and respond to
the good news and accept that the Messiah has truly come to save us
and to reveal His love that surpasses all human understanding.

Ponder
2 Corinthians 3:7–18

Question to consider
• Why not pray today that the Lord would unveil the hearts and
  minds of the people you know, so that they can truly know the
  risen King?

Reflect
Read aloud Isaiah 43:1–13 as a proclamation of what you believe.

DAY 30

The Saviour and Redeemer

Opening prayer

Father, thank You for paying the price for my sin on the cross and loving me so much that I can have a relationship with You. Please strengthen me to love like You do. Amen.

Bible reading

Luke 2:11,30

Jesus came to save us from death, to redeem us from the grave. Our sin and fallen nature meant that we were left distant from the Lord. God's work on the cross, shedding His blood, was redemptive in that His death was a price that He paid to bring us back into relationship with Him. His love was so awesome, so sacrificial, a free gift to all the world – a saving love that washes us clean and takes us into the inner sanctuary with Jesus. The Saviour and Redeemer that we encounter in Christ truly takes my breath away!

As we are transformed by Christ's unconditional love, we find that the love that we have for others becomes less conditional. The Spirit transforms our hearts so that we can forgive those who have hurt us and love our enemy more easily. Jesus longs for us to share His saving, redeeming love with others, through loving like He did … although this can be so challenging!

Martin Luther King, Jr. challenges us with this, 'Love has within it a redemptive power. And there is a power there that eventually transforms individuals. Just keep being friendly to that person. Just keep loving them, and they can't stand it too long. Oh, they react in many ways in the beginning. They react with guilt feelings, and sometimes they'll hate you a little more at that transition period, but just keep loving them. And by the power of your love they will break down under the load. That's love, you see. It is redemptive, and this is why Jesus says love.'*

When you consider the people that you struggle with, it is really hard to accept that Christ came to save them too. Someone challenged me recently to pray for a person who had hurt me badly but at first I found it impossible. However, the more I have grasped the saving love of Jesus in my life, the easier it is to ask God to touch their life.

The old saying 'an eye for an eye, a tooth for a tooth' or 'you reap what you sow' is not what Jesus wants for His children. He doesn't abandon us even when we abandon Him. He hasn't paid us back for our sin by remaining far from us. Jesus' death and resurrection achieves the exact opposite – loving us, inviting us, sacrificing for us, *despite* what we have done. It leaves us challenged to think about our relationships, to wonder at Christ's love, and to ask for His help in loving us despite the choices and behaviour of other people. With the Spirit's power and strength we can model Jesus and reveal His love.

Ponder
Job 19:25; Ruth 4:13–22

Questions to consider
• Are there people who you struggle to love?
• Is there anyone you have given up loving because it is too difficult?
• Jesus has forgiven us for everything we have ever done or will do – can you forgive too?
• Is it time to stop looking to 'pay back' and instead release the hurt in a loving way?

Reflect
Read the Lord's Prayer from Matthew 6:9–15, asking God to help you with verse 14.

*Edited by Peter Holloran, *A Knock at Midnight: Inspiration from the Great Sermons of Reverend Martin Luther King, Jr.* (Warner Books, 2000)

DAY 31

A living testimony

Opening prayer

Heavenly Father, thank You that we are letters of testimony to You; not written with ink but with the Spirit of the living God. Please take us and transform us to write Your truth on human hearts. Amen.

Bible reading

Luke 1:1–4

As this Advent season draws to a close, let's finish where we began by remembering those Gospel authors who faithfully attempted to write the truth about Christ. Luke tells us that, 'Many have undertaken to draw up an account of the things that have been fulfilled among us, just as they were handed down to us by those who from the first were eyewitnesses and servants of the word' (vv1–2). In Luke's time, many individuals were living lives wanting to share the truth about Jesus. Many were trying to pass this eternal story down the generations because they were so powerfully impacted by the gospel.

Still today we write with a longing in our hearts and a narrative that will last for all time; Jesus is the Son of God and we will serve Him with everything that we have until He takes us home. The question remains – who are we living for? Are we setting our sights on earthly dreams that will fade away? Are we prioritising everything other than Jesus in our daily pattern of living? Or are we intent on passing on the Christ story to the people that we live amongst?

Jesus longed that we would go and make disciples of all nations (Matt. 28:19). He promises to go with us and that we will see Him move in power by His Holy Spirit. His heart's cry is that we will be sheep who know a Shepherd, hearing His voice and doing what He asks us to do. He declares that we will have life in all its fullness because we know Him, 'the author of life'. This King and Lord is our God and if we remain in Him, we will bear much fruit; apart from Him we can do nothing.

The world will tell us to strive for money, for a sense of belonging, to look as good and as young as we possibly can. The media will encourage us to work for worldly recognition and fame. But our Lord says, 'Be still and know that I am God' (Psa. 46:10). Jesus tells Martha to stop running around and to do what Mary is doing, because she is sitting and listening to everything Jesus is saying (Luke 10:39). We know too that Jesus took time to be with His Father (Mark 1:35). Do you need to rest more with the Lord?

Next year, spend time alone with your heavenly Father listening and being still in His presence. During this time, the Lord will show you what to do and where He is calling you to make disciples. May you know the blessing of the Father, the Son and the Holy Spirit in all the days ahead.

Ponder
2 Corinthians 3:1–6

Questions to consider
- Are you more of a 'do-er' than a 'rester', or the other way round?
- How does the Lord want to change the way you live?
- Why not think of a couple of people who you would like to encounter Christ next year and begin to pray for opportunities to share the love of God with them?

Reflect
Read Exodus 14:14, praying that you can 'let go and let God'.

Group Study Notes

On the following pages you will find suggestions for group study for each of the four sections contained in this study guide. The overall aim of these studies is to draw every person in your group closer to God's beloved Son, Jesus Christ, by digging deeper into the Word of God. These group sections are focused on the same passages that have been examined in the individual Bible studies, so they will build on what has already been considered in the daily readings. However, if you haven't studied the individual reflections, the summary sections should give you enough understanding to participate.

Each group study includes a short recap of the entire section's daily notes, an opening Bible reading, six discussion starters and a final Bible reading to close the study. Each discussion starter indicates which day the question arises from, if you wish to refer back.

Please feel free to use the material in a way that suits your group, perhaps picking out certain questions for discussion or adding your own, and injecting times of quiet or worship where desired. Members of the group may wish to discuss something that came up in the section that is not covered in these discussion starters, or you may find that you spend a lot of time on just one question – that is fine; there is no obligation to complete the entire study!

My prayer is that you and your group will have powerful individual and social times of encountering Christ, understanding more of His truth and be able to apply it to your life today. Enjoy!

ONE: PREPARE THE WAY

In this first section we have turned to the incredible Gospel authors Matthew and Luke, examining their faithful insight into the Christmas story and how Zechariah and Elizabeth's pregnancy prepares us for the arrival of the King. We have been encouraged to think about the righteous nature of Zechariah, asking ourselves if we struggle with doubt and fear in our own walk with Christ. Elizabeth helps rebuild our confidence and belief that, with God, anything is possible!

Read
Matthew 1:1–25; Luke 1:1–25

Discuss
1. Do you have a regular time that you carve out to spend with the Lord? If not, why not? Would you like to change your pattern? (Day 1)
2. How do you feel about trusting God with everything? Are there aspects of your life where you like to stay in control? (Day 3)
3. What is your deepest fear? Does it affect your daily decisions? Together, ask Jesus to break the cycle of fear in your life. (Day 4)
4. Elizabeth found that nothing was impossible with God. Is there anyone in the group who has lost hope? Pray for them that their faith would rise again, despite their circumstances. (Day 5)
5. Have you witnessed God's perfect timing? Perhaps you can share testimonies of when you have seen answered prayer, in a way that suddenly made sense … it may have only been seen with the benefit of hindsight! (Day 6)
6. Share together a couple of things for which you are truly thankful to God. Praise God for these things in your lives. (Day 7)

End the group time by reading Psalm 48 together as a declaration of who the Lord truly is. Ask one member of the group to conclude in prayer.

TWO: DRAW NEAR TO JESUS

In this second section we have delved deeper into the lives of Mary, Joseph and Simeon, exploring what they teach us about how we can draw near to Jesus. We discover the importance of putting Jesus first, listening to His voice, staying faithful and realising that He loves us and is calling every one of us to walk with Him.

Read
Luke 1:26–38; 2:25–35; Matthew 1:18–25

Discuss
1. Share with one another what or who is your greatest priority and why. If you had to make a list, where would Jesus be on it? Second place, third, or top priority? (Day 8)
2. How do people in your group feel about being 'highly favoured' by God? Do they believe it? Encourage those who find it hard (perhaps use scriptures like Isa. 43:4). (Day 9)
3. Are there areas of your life that you need the power of the Spirit to break in? Discuss together. (Day 10)
4. Spend a minute thinking about the last time that you encountered Christ (it may have been when you became a Christian). How did it affect your life? (Day 11)
5. Have you ever felt prompted to give anything up (perhaps over Lent)? What difference did it make to your walk with God? (Day 12)
6. How do you feel about waiting for something? Are you patient? Are there people present who have been waiting for a long time? (Day 15)

Ask one person to read Proverbs 8:32–35 out loud, then move into a time of quiet, waiting on the Lord. Give space to share thoughts then conclude with a prayer that the Lord will be close to those who are waiting for Him.

THREE: SEEK HIM FIRST

In this third section we contemplated the importance of Christ in everything. Focusing on Anna's intimacy with the Lord and the magi's journey encourages us to be actively seeking our King and to be careful about what we do and where we look for Him. The shepherds highlight that Christ reveals Himself to us all.

Read
Luke 2:8–20,36–38; Matthew 2:1–16

Discuss
1. Have you been making more space for God since beginning these studies? What have been the challenges in doing this? (Day 16)
2. Being honest, are there particular ages or generations that you are more prone to ignore? How can we work together to love and notice them more? (Day 17)
3. Share and encourage each other in the different roles that individuals play, however big or small they may feel. How do the things we do, however small, bless others? (Day 18)
4. How do the group feel about sharing their faith? Does anyone have a testimony of a positive encounter with someone of another, or no, faith? Perhaps there are opportunities coming up at church soon that you can invite people to? (Day 20)
5. Share your dreams with one another. What are the things that you long to do or see in your lifetime (Day 21)
6. Ask the group whether they feel like they are: in a valley, up a mountain, at a dead end, crossing a river, or in another place? (You could use a picture or map and ask people to mark where they are.)

Using the responses from question 6, pray for one another (perhaps in pairs), asking for the Lord to minister into each situation.

FOUR: WHO WILL YOU LIVE FOR?

In this final section we consider Herod's state of mind and his devastating decisions. We are also encouraged to examine our own hearts and ponder whether we are acting out of a pure heart, motivated by Christ's love. Finally, we consider the author of our lives, Jesus – who He is and what He has done for us.

Read
Matthew 2; Luke 1:1–4,32; 2:10,30–35

Discuss
1. Consider the fruit of the Spirit in Galatians 5. Ask the group which one they find the most challenging and why. (Day 24)
2. What do you want to build in your lifetime? What would you want written on your gravestone? (Day 25)
3. Imagine a cup, overflowing with God's love. Now picture yourself as that cup. How full do you feel? Are you running on empty? Pray for those who need more of Christ's love. (Day 26)
4. Who do you know that needs Christ to be the Good Shepherd of their lives? Pray for them that they would be found by Jesus and drawn into His flock. (Day 28)
5. Are there people that you find it difficult to love? Do you pray for them? How can you 'just keep loving them' as Martin Luther King, Jr. said? (Day 30)
6. Over the last 31 days, what has challenged you the most from this Advent study and group conversations? Share with one another what difference it will make to your life in the months ahead (Day 31)

Finish by praying together and thanking the Lord for who He is and all He has shown you over this time.

Cover to Cover Bible Studies for Lent

NEW TITLE

At the Cross
by Abby Guinness

Consider the experiences of six Bible characters who witnessed the crucifixion. Their stories and responses can help us find fresh perspective on the death and resurrection of Jesus and the wider implications of what was achieved for us personally and as a human race. Discover a creative approach to exploring the Bible, with textual and historical insights alongside group discussion topics and personal application.

72-page booklet, 210x148mm
ISBN: 978-1-78259-498-7

Fleeting Shadows
by Malcolm Duncan

Malcolm Duncan draws from his own life experience to help us reflect on the cross and the power of Christ as we walk through challenging trials and tribulations.

72-page booklet, 210x148mm
ISBN: 978-1-78259-420-8

Centred on Christ
by Michael Baughen

Explore the peace of a Christ-centred life when we learn to rejoice in Christ and not in circumstances.

72-page booklet, 210x148mm
ISBN: 978-1-78259-017-0

To find out about all our Lent titles, for current prices and to order visit
www.cwr.org.org.uk/store
Available online or from Christian bookshops.

smallGroup central

All of our small group ideas and resources in one place

Online:

www.smallgroupcentral.org.uk
is filled with free video teaching, tools, articles and a whole host of ideas.

On the road:

A range of seminars themed for small groups can be brought to your local community. Contact us at **hello@smallgroupcentral.org.uk**

In print:

Books, study guides and DVDs covering an extensive list of themes, Bible books and life issues.

vital:

cover to cover

Every Day with Jesus extra

Liz Babbs STUDY GUIDE

40 DAYS WITH JESUS

Life JOURNEYS

ToolBox

Log on and find out more at:
www.smallgroupcentral.org.uk

Courses and events

Waverley Abbey College

Publishing and media

Conference facilities

Transforming lives

CWR's vision is to enable people to experience personal transformation through applying God's Word to their lives and relationships.

Our Bible-based training and resources help people around the world to:
• Grow in their walk with God
• Understand and apply Scripture to their lives
• Resource themselves and their church
• Develop pastoral care and counselling skills
• Train for leadership
• Strengthen relationships, marriage and family life and much more.

Our insightful writers provide daily Bible reading notes and other resources for all ages, and our experienced course designers and presenters have gained an international reputation for excellence and effectiveness.

CWR's Training and Conference Centres in Surrey and East Sussex, England, provide excellent facilities in idyllic settings – ideal for both learning and spiritual refreshment.

 Applying God's Word
to everyday life and relationships

CWR, Waverley Abbey House,
Waverley Lane, Farnham,
Surrey GU9 8EP, UK

Telephone: **+44 (0)1252 784700**
Email: info@cwr.org.uk
Website: www.cwr.org.uk

Registered Charity No. 294387
Company Registration No. 1990308